Kill the Goblins!

How to get the negative voices in your head to shut-up

By

Miranda K

First Printing: 15th May 2023

Published by Purple Queen Publishing

Paperback ISBN: 978-90-832140-5-4
Ebook ISBN: 978-90-8321-40-6-1

Disclaimer

I am not a trained therapist or psychologist.

What I am providing in this book is based on my own experience as someone who has been through a great deal of childhood abuse, including physical, sexual, emotional and verbal abuse, and spent years in therapy finding ways to process and recover from it.

I have been diagnosed as someone suffering Complex PTSD (Post Traumatic Stress Disorder), which is a constant stream of trauma rather than a single event. But I have not at any point trained to be a trauma specialist.

Nothing in this book offers any form of diagnosis or treatment, it is simply a book of strategies and tools that worked for me and might help others alongside any other treatment or therapies conducted by professionals in their respective fields.

Contents

"Goblins are born when you're wounded and something essential is lost in that experience. From that point on, as you forget your wholeness, they remain with you in the shadows. There they remind you of what brought them into being, by mimicking your own voice, tricking you into believing that you're unworthy, victimised, or unlovable."

The Enchanted Map, Oracle Cards
by Colette Baron-Reid,
Card No.5: Goblins.

Why this book?

"A tongue has no bones but it can break a heart."
Proverb

Out of the abuse I suffered throughout my child-hood, the verbal abuse was the most pervasive. From the age of eleven upwards, after my siblings had left home and I was alone with my single parent, the daily diatribe about why I wasn't important and why I was a burden screamed at me daily worked its way deep into my psyche. It imprinted on my sub-conscious, becoming a part of my internal dialogue that would repeat continuously after I left home at eighteen years of age. It caused disruption in every aspect of my life: relationships, friendships, and working life.

A series of nightly panic attacks in my early twen-ties that went on for six months, sent me into two rounds of therapy (twelve sessions each) where I learned some tools to try and find a balance again. Then somewhere in my late twenties, after terming myself 'neurotic' in a conversation, someone told me that the only person who thought I was neurotic was myself, and I started to become conscious of my negative internal dialogue and the negative scenarios I would enact in my mind: imagined arguments and conflicts with people around me. I realised it was ever-present, feeding my paranoia and envy of others, and leaving me feeling wrong, out of place, and disconnected.

After a breakdown at the end of my thirties caused by pressures in my external life (becoming a new parent, wife and being a social group leader) created a 'noise' of paranoid thoughts and voices in my head which reached fever pitch, I sought more help and returned to therapy, this time for six years. There I finally unravelled the voices that fed the negative internal dialogue and the cause that generated their arrival.

Up until this point I hadn't thought my noisy mind was abnormal, but my therapist assured me it was indicative of a person living in high stress, introducing the idea that it was actually possible to quiet my mind. They helped me learn systems that I could put in place to break and stop them – if only for a moment – and change their trajectory from becoming overwhelming.

It's taken a good ten years of solid, consistent and active work to reach this point, and I still can have days when the 'goblins' invade – a name I came across for the negative voices in my head when dabbling in oracle cards. Coined by Colette Baron-Reid in her Oracle Map Deck on card No. 5 (see the quote at the opening), she captured the essence of those voices in that name; describing the destructive trouble makers bent on causing mischief in the form of self-doubt, self-questioning, sabotaging self-trust and self-assurance.

Over those ten years I realised that the strategies I had developed weren't just helpful to me on my 'noisy head' days, but to friends who also suffered. And when one of them suggested they might be useful to a wider audience, I decided it was time to put them in a book.

This book is written in two parts: the first covers the in-the-moment strategies that can divert your thinking at the point when you become conscious of negative internal dialogue; the second is for those looking to go deeper and try and uncover the layers behind the voices. The first part is for managing the symptoms; the second is for uncovering the root cause.

Take what works and leave the rest. This is simply a tool and a starting point.

A word about retraining your thinking

"Whatever you hold in your mind on a consistent basis is exactly what you will experience in your life."
Tony Robbins

Retraining the way you think isn't easy, it requires determination and persistence. It's about becoming conscious of what you are thinking on a daily basis, being aware of what is coming up in your conscious mind and observing it, rather than reacting to it.

Even in my teens when I was alone with my single parent, and they were letting loose on me with their life frustrations and making me the cause of them, I was aware it was possible to change how you thought and how you perceived life. I could observe my parent from an outside standpoint and see the mental patterns they were caught up in and repeating, and where they originated. I always believed it was just a matter of being able to see things from another perspective – however hard that might be in the moment.

It wasn't until I was older that I began to understand how difficult it would be to actually implement retraining my thoughts, because the older you get the busier your life becomes, and you don't have the time to focus on your own behaviours and reactions, and unearth the thought processes and reroute them.

You have to go deeper to pull out the rotten core of what has been planted in your subconscious. Because it is that that feeds the conscious mind, and they run in an endless loop, until you break the conscious stream and literally replace the thoughts and words, and persistently do this, until one day your subconscious automatically starts throwing up those replacement thoughts and words automatically when you are having a bad day, to counter the negativity.

Yes, it can actually happen. It now happens to me quite a lot. I would say it has taken about ten years of consistent work.

But I didn't realise my ability or knowing that I could retrain my thinking was unique. It seems most people didn't have that kind of awareness and ability to self-reflect – certainly not at a young age. I believed everyone could do this, and they can, but for some (like my single parent) it can feel like an insurmountable task.

And it is exhausting, on a day-to-day basis having to constantly safeguard against falling prey to the negative internal dialogue. But I want you to know it IS possible; I have, for the most part, achieved it. And now, standing on the other side of what I refer to as a wall, one which I ploughed through to get here, it is totally worth it.

I do still read a LOT of self-help books (a guilty pleasure of mine) and still follow several of the strategies outlined in this book. But my mind is quieter. I am calmer in my thinking, and I feel more emotionally balanced.

Avoiding jargon

"Words of the jargon sound as if they said something higher than what they mean." Theodor W. Adorno

I'm conscious of how terminology in the self-help, personal development and mental health world has corroded the global view on such topics. A lot of it slips into buzz words and terms, and sometimes further into the spiritual or esoteric (woo woo) arena — such as 'law of attraction'. Because of that a stigma has developed and attached to this kind of book and this kind of information. People shun it just by seeing certain terms or wording.

Plus a lot of the terminology has become overly complicated and not very helpful. I endeavour to use what I call layman's terms: simple, straight forward words that make it more accessible and understandable for those that don't spend much time being absorbed in it (as I have), and just need help.

Part One
Handling the Goblins

Introduction to Part One

The following chapters provide 'in-the-moment strategies'. They are things you can do to stop a stream of negative internal dialogue – whatever that looks like for you: an imagined catastrophe or imagined argument, berating yourself in your mind over something, or just generally not saying nice things to yourself.

The key identifier of negative internal dialogue is that it leaves you feeling bad about yourself, whether it's something from the past or a potential future event.

These strategies aim to help you stop doing that and even find a way to turn it around. There is no special sequence or preference, just read them through and try any that you think might help you.

Also feel free to adapt them to suit you, your lifestyle, and your needs. Every person is different and each person responds differently. Don't feel you have to copy them exactly, they are open to alteration and your own personal interpretation.

And remember, none of these are magic pills that will stop it permanently. Fighting the negative voices is an ongoing thing. You may reach a point – as I have – where it is significantly reduced with just a few bad days from time to time. But it takes vigilance and conscious work to interrupt and change your thinking.

Be compassionate to yourself like you would a friend or loved one, and remember that if you are reading this you have already started to take the steps towards recovering your peace of mind.

Saying 'Stop'

"Be careful how you talk to yourself,
because you are listening."
Lisa M Hayes

This strategy is for the moments when you become conscious of your negative internal dialogue. You interrupt it the moment you realise it is happening.

Once you become aware that you are saying stuff in your head that is bringing on a physical emotional reaction: making you feel sick, anxious, angry, or sad, you break it by saying 'Stop', either out loud or in your mind.

I tend to follow up with saying to myself, "thinking this is not helpful to you, the only person you are hurting, upsetting, or persecuting is yourself."

I also sometimes ask myself if any of what I am imagining or saying to myself is true, or likely to happen. Often the response is no. I will then follow up with asking myself why I am thinking this: how am I feeling? What is really upsetting me?

If you aren't saying nice things to yourself, or you're berating yourself, ask yourself, if a stranger came up to you on the street and said those things to you, how would you feel? If a friend of yours said those things to you, how would you feel? And ask yourself again why you are saying those things to yourself.

To connect to ourselves we must become friends with ourselves. We need to find compassion, and care about how we feel as we would friends or family – you can't get more family than yourself.

Of course this is based in self-worth and if you feel you aren't worth anything or good enough this will be a struggle. But those voices in your head, that negative dialogue, it feeds those words – and it is also fed by those words in a sort of continuous loop, like a snake eating its own tail. When you break that loop by interrupting those words, you stop it being automatic or habitual; you change the thought process by questioning it and/or reframing it.

Reframing means saying the same thing but from another perspective. For example, negative internal dialogue stream:

"I wasn't a good mum/dad today. I'm never a good mum/dad. My kids are better off without me."

Or:

"I wasn't a good friend today. I'm never a good friend. No wonder I don't have any friends."

Reframing:

"Today was a difficult day. I could have done better as a mum/dad today. Tomorrow I will do better. Everyone has bad days. How about going to give my kids a hug, so we can all feel better?"

Or:

"I really struggled with being a good friend today. I was mean/hard on my friend today. That's not who I am. I'll go and give them a call/send them a message and apologise."

Notice that I have given add-ons to the reframing; it's not just the sentence but a solution to help yourself feel better and reconnect, either to someone or to yourself. That might not be possible in the moment, but they are an example of how you can carry it through later.

Initially don't worry about the reframing, the main priority in this strategy is to stop the negative chain of dialogue and divert your thinking.

It doesn't matter how many times you need to do this. It doesn't matter if you don't always manage to succeed. It's all about becoming aware of what you are saying to yourself that is hurtful or unhelpful — that alone will change it.

The more often you stop these thoughts, the less power they will have over you; the less they will control your mind. They will reduce, and they will change.

Persistence is key.

It's okay to have a day where you realised you haven't managed it, or you feel particularly overwhelmed by your negative thoughts. You haven't failed. You only fail when you give up.

Don't give up, you're worth it – as is your peace of mind. Every day is a new day and an opportunity to start afresh and try again.

Writing it out

"Journal writing is a voyage to the interior."
Christina Baldwin

I'm a writer (of fiction as well as non-fiction) so for me journaling is my first go to. Whenever I get upset, overwhelmed, or want to try and work out why I am feeling the way I do, I turn to my journal. It's where I express everything I feel, good or bad, and where I try and find solutions to how I feel.

You can choose any method you like from keeping a diary and writing in it daily about whatever is bothering you or upsetting you, or something more committed and specific like Morning Pages, where you write three pages every morning about anything that is on your mind when you wake up, like writing down your conscious stream. Or you can journal sporadically when you have the most need and something is bothering you, although I would recommend trying to make it a habit of say at least three times a week. Consider it checking in on yourself and how you are feeling – because that's what you are doing.

You can chose to have different journals for different things. I have one for my friends and one for my marriage. I use a different one when I want to focus on something. I have one for a course I followed about listening to my heart, and another for a course on learning to love myself, which include different exercises every day.

A journal is all about you. It's not for anyone else to read – unless you want them to. It's about getting any bad feelings off your chest, and working through anything you find difficult. I often find the solutions to things when I write them out. I ask all the questions that frustrate me, about events or people. You can even write all the angry stuff and burn it if you like, make a ritual of it to release it.

The very process of writing things out takes it out of your head and puts it somewhere where you can observe it. I have found it very helpful to look back over the years and see the patterns of thinking, the thoughts and feelings that circulate the most, and realise where I still need to make changes. It also enables me to see how far I have come and where I have been able to make progress.

Connecting with yourself in this way helps you understand yourself better. It enables you to see inside yourself and explore thoughts and feelings which influence your external life. Through this process you listen to your feelings and learn to trust them – and thus trust yourself.

So go out and buy yourself a special journal or notebook (or a couple of them) and some pens you love using that has a special ink colour (I use purple Bic biros) and see if writing it out helps you.

And if you open that first page and you don't know where to start, maybe ask yourself some questions like:

How do I feel today?

What's on my mind today?

Or, I don't know what I am feeling today.

A journal is for you to write everything and anything, and to say whatever is on your mind.

Sing and Dance

"Music can heal the wounds which medicine cannot touch."
Debasish Mridha

Sing is not just a Disney movie, it's an action that has been medically proven to help those who suffer with mental health. Singing releases endorphins, which are feel-good hormones, and a tiny organ in the ear called the sacculus responds pleasurably to the frequencies created by singing.

It also changes how you breathe, causing you to breathe more slowly and deeply. The process of exhalation stimulates the parasympathetic nervous system (the part of the body that enables rest and digestion, unlike the sympathetic nervous system that is triggered by reaction.)

"Singing is a form of regular, controlled breathing, since breathing out occurs on the song phrases

and inhaling takes place between these. It gives you pretty much the same effect as yoga breathing. It helps you relax, and there are indications that it does provide a heart benefit."

Dr Björn Vickhoff, a musicologist at the University of Gothenburg in Sweden

The other thing it does is distract, particularly from overthinking or from a noisy mind. As your subconscious mind is thinking about how to breathe, and your conscious mind is concentrating on the words or sounds you are making, it's not able to overrun itself with thoughts about anything else.

And it doesn't matter whether you think you can sing or not, or what you sing, or where you sing. Sing for yourself and the pleasure of the feeling. Even if only for one song.

It can also be a great way to connect with people though – and I don't just mean at a Karaoke night. If you have small children, it's a great way to have fun. I still remember my son's shocked expression when he was about five years old and kept calling, "Mama, mama" at me and I burst into song with 'Mama Mia' by Abba. It also helped us laugh together too.

Singing anything and everything will help you get past shame and embarrassment, and elevate your self-esteem. Even if you think you are out of tune, it won't matter, it's about finding pleasure in the moment and not allowing the negative internal dialogue to take over.

You can even deliberately sing out of tune and laugh with it. It will help you let go of bad feelings about yourself or other people as you regulate your emotions and lift them. It will change your perspective and hopefully enable you to view things in a brighter light.

For more about the science behind how singing works to alleviate stress in the body, it relates to the Vagus nerve, the longest cranial nerve in the body. It's connected to the vocal cords and the back of the throat, and also other organs, playing an important part in the parasympathetic nervous system, which affects your heart rate among other things.

Singing stimulates the Vagus nerve causing the heart rate to slow. Studies have also found there's a release of oxytocin into the body when singing, which has a calming effect on the body. (Oxytocin is also known as the 'love hormone', and is released during hugging.)

And often when we sing, we move too. Changing our physical state also changes our mental state, so some form of dancing, anywhere you can in the moment – even in the car, you can still bounce up and down as you turn the music up full blast to flush out the nasty chatter from the goblins in your head.

It enables you to take a break from your thoughts and a moment to experience something joyful, and for an in-the-moment strategy that is the aim.

Set A Review Date

*"There is nothing in this world that can trouble you
as much as your own mind."*
Sri Sri Ravi Shankar

This is a strategy my therapist gave me. I had a particular problem in that I became consumed with trying to find a way out of my situation. It was ALL I ever thought about from the second I woke up until the moment I went to sleep, and it was not only affecting my mental health (it was part of my breakdown in 2008) but was affecting my ability to parent, as well as engage with people and the life around me. I didn't want to be there, I wanted to be somewhere else – anywhere else, but I couldn't due to financial reasons, logistical reasons (living in a foreign country) and being a mum. But yet every day I taxed myself with the problem, going over and over it. It affected my mood: I was defensive, frustrated and quick to anger. It left me feeling powerless and drained.

Until one day my therapist asked me if I was actually going to change my living situation that year. I answered no. They said, okay then, set a date next year when you are going to review this, and then every time you find yourself thinking about it, you say to yourself, no, I'm not going to think about that until such-and-such date and refuse to engage with further thoughts on it. Take a holiday from it. Give yourself a mental break.

When I began to implement this, it wasn't easy, but after a while I found myself thinking less and less about my frustration with being unable to get out of my situation. I stopped focusing on it so much, I began to see and appreciate the life I did have around me. I was able to put myself in the present moment and embrace it.

It gave me room to breathe mentally and help work on other issues. It helped me look at what I had through another perspective and return some of my sense of personal power and autonomy over my life. And now, although I am still in the situation, I have been able to make changes within it that have enabled me to enjoy life and pursue things that are important to me and give me a sense of worth.

People say there's no point worrying about something if you can't do anything about it, but it's easier said than done. And especially in situations where you want to be able to do something but you can't, for whatever reason, it can become overwhelming. But continuing to push up against something you can't change only drains you and becomes a form of self-persecution.

By giving yourself the option to put off the worry means you can give yourself mental space, and occasionally within that space it allows solutions to arise. Either way you're able to restore a sense of balance to your life and your thinking.

So if you find yourself with a problem or situation you can't do anything about, or you can't change in that moment (or day, week, month or year), rather than go over and over it, ask yourself if you can defer that worry and take a mental break from it.

Set a date – it can be for any time length, and when you find the goblins in your mind bringing it up and you start wrangling this particular problem again, interrupt them and remind them you aren't going to think about it until that date. Argue with them if you have to, but persist in refusing to entertain any of the chatter on the topic until the review date you have set.

And what happens when you get to that date? Literally review it: Has anything changed? Can you do anything about your particularly problem now? If so, then do it, if not, then set another date.

The idea is to give yourself mental space to be and think and, most importantly, to stop that incessant chatter in your head that leaves you feeling powerless.

And you can use this strategy again and again, however many times you need it.

Helpful Questions

Often when the goblins have overrun my thoughts and I become overwhelmed, the negative emotions they create start to drive me into what I call 'victim' thinking. I start asking myself things like: 'Why does it always happen to me? What is wrong with me? What am I doing wrong? What have I done to deserve this?'

These are unhelpful questions. The answers to them only lead into further negative dialogue of blame, shame, and torturous thoughts as I try and justify or reason all the things I think are bad about myself. It continues on into a never-ending downward spiral creating worse states of mind.

These questions make the assumption that there is something wrong with me; that I am at fault in some way if things aren't working out. This is simply not true. They ask questions that give no solution to the problem and disempower me.

The strategy to combat this in the moment is re-framing those questions. I mentioned reframing thoughts in the chapter 'Saying 'Stop''. It involves changing perspective and point of view, looking at something another way, and approaching it from a different angle. It's possible to do this with these questions by changing them and making them 'helpful'.

In this instance 'helpful' would mean questions that enable you to think about what the truth is, how you can feel better, even bring up some solutions to whatever it is that is causing you to ask them in the first place. But primarily to take the pressure off whatever situation or chain of thought is driving this thought process.

Let's have a look at some examples of helpful questions:

- ❖ How am I feeling right now?

- ❖ Why am I feeling this way?

- ❖ What is the lesson here?

- ❖ How can I learn from this?

- ❖ How can I do things differently?

❖ What small steps can I take today to feel better?

All of these are open questions and offer a way for you to think about what you can do to help yourself or find compassion for yourself, and take action towards whatever you feel you need to do or change.

They don't strip you, they empower you. They give you the feeling that you can do something constructive giving you a starting point and sense of purpose. It stops the mind from slipping into more negative thoughts about yourself and feeding the goblins, allowing them to grow.

So next time you find yourself with those questions try and turn them around. For example:

Instead of saying: 'What have I done wrong?'

Ask: 'What can I do differently?'

Instead of saying: 'What is wrong with me?'

Ask: 'Why is this situation not working for me?'

Instead of saying: 'What have I done to deserve this?'

Ask: 'What is the lesson in this?'

No matter what the original question, if it only leads you to feel bad, query it. Ask yourself if it is a helpful question or an unhelpful question. Ask yourself how you can think differently and what question would help you think differently.

The point here is to distract the mind from further unhelpful thinking, and change the internal dialogue you are using with yourself, moving to a more constructive way of thinking.

You might not be able to manage it every time, but even if you only recognise you were thinking that way after the fact, you have become conscious that you were doing it, and that is a win, a step in the right direction.

Visualisation

Visualisation is a broad term for many things. People talk about visualising what you want, or creating a visualisation board of pictures to help you imagine what you want and focus on it. And you can do that, but in this instance I am talking about using visualisation as a strategy to address the goblins or the negative voices in your head, directly.

You can choose to visualise the voices as a person – or a goblin – or whoever/whatever you feel is behind the negative internal dialogue; the person who first said the things to you that you are now repeating to yourself. Or you can visualise the feeling that the words make you feel.

You can do this a multitude of ways: much like journaling, you can write it out or draw it out, creating a physical drawing of what you imagine the goblins in your head look like, or what a particular bad feeling looks like. Or you can just simply bring them to mind either as an imagined person or an actual person that you believe put that voice in your head, and then you talk to it.

Yes, that's what I said, talk to it. You can do this out loud or keep it in your mind, but address it as though you were having a conversation with them.

You can even make a ritual of it. I used to take a photo of the person who I had in my mind saying nasty things to me (mostly it was my single parent, but sometimes it was an ex-partner or old friend), and I'd put it next to a lit candle, and I'd stare into the flame as I brought them to mind.

I'd see them in my mind's eye: how they would walk and talk, seeing snapshots of interactions with them in my mind. Then I would say everything I felt, all the things I had bottled up inside and never said to them in person – or never would say to them in person. It would help me release the feelings I had, and give me closure. I would imagine them listening to me.

I would, however, be very careful NOT to imagine a response.

In these visualisation, the purpose of them is to resolve your feelings, your pain, as a way to reduce the noise in your head and recover your peace of mind. This process is not about the other person, or what they might think, say, or feel about anything you are expressing in this imagined conversation. It is solely for you to let go of all the pent up emotions you have felt that are behind the negative voices in your head. If anything, I would imagine them just standing there and taking it.

Feel free to be angry and even shout at them, whatever works for you. I would even sometimes imagine putting my single parent into the flame of the candle and burning them up on days where I was overwhelmed with my feelings of anger and hurt.

But visualisation techniques can be quite difficult for some people. There are people who can't visualise things. You might even be one of them. Not all people can see in pictures, they see in words. I am a visual person, in my mind I see in pictures and they inform both my internal world and external world. But for some people it doesn't work that way, they see in words.

If that is the case for you, you can try writing a letter to that person, voice, or goblin, and express yourself that way. You can even write out a single emotion, maybe use a different colour pen or crayon to express the feeling. Or just let your own feelings out verbally using those words. Shout at them if required, whatever works for you.

This strategy can be something you can take time over or something you can do in the moment. If a voice pops up in your mind with something nasty or snarky to say, you can tell it where it can go in a simple two-word form – or multiple, get as creative as you like. Whatever helps you feel like you are in control and have power over it – because you do.

Either way the purpose is to relieve you of the negative effects of this chatter, and break the cycle of these repetitive thought processes that leave you emotionally affected.

Prioritise

*"I am not a product of my circumstances.
I am a product of my decisions."*
Stephen R Covey

A lot of the noise in my head gets caused by over-whelm, which means when I have a lot of things to do and I can't decide where to start and I struggle to focus. Then the goblins like to start reminding me how I am always procrastinating and I can never follow through and how I should feel bad about myself – you know how it goes. So this in-the-moment strategy looks at how to change that.

A common question I've been asked by people who are struggling with a long list of day-to-day chores as well as work demands, is 'how do I get started?'

Here I am going to provide two strategies: one that works well in the moment and one that might take you a bit longer, but I urge you to consider doing the longer one to get a bit of distance and perspective on just how much you do in any given day or week.

The short version of this is to write a list of the things you want to do that day; write them down as they come out of your head, then strike through all them except the top one and ONLY focus on that top one until it is done, and then do the same again.

It is important to actually rewrite that list, because your mind will always put first what is at the forefront of your mind; the one item that you want to get done. Some people avoid the most pressing item because it might be bigger than the rest. You might want to get the easy things over first. But try and go with this method and see how you get on.

When you have a noisy head full of goblins it can be hard to get your mind to concentrate on one task, but there is no such thing as multi-tasking, there is only multi-failing. It might be possible to do one thing while listening to something else depending what the physical task is – I find it perfectly possible to clean the bathroom while listening to my weekly podcast because cleaning doesn't require a lot of mental thought processes, many of them are automated, much like watching your favourite film or TV show while ironing.

But trying to write while listening to someone else talking is a bit more difficult, or going through the weekly budget while watching the latest episode of favourite series; you are going to either take twice as long doing either one (having to rewind the podcast or episode), or you won't have paid attention to one of the tasks properly and might have a problem later.

Putting your mind to just one job gets you in the habit of applying yourself to one thing at a time. And you will have a great deal of satisfaction at striking that item off your list, and later the pride in knowing you have completed it and a boost to your confidence at having followed through. All things necessary to shut those goblins up.

The larger strategy, one that I find helpful when finding myself struggling on a regular basis, is when you review ALL the things you do. They can be anything related to chores at home, your tasks at work, even your relationship. In fact I got this idea from a book called, Have The Relationship You Want, by Rori Raye, and have since adapted it to look at what I am expecting from myself, and reviewing it.

Here's the step by step:

List all the things you do – include everything, no matter how small, it is all significant. (This might take several pages.)

Then go through the list, marking each one with a priority number of 1-4:

1 – I must do

2 – I must do, but it's not as important

3 – I can delegate to someone else

4 – This is not for me

This should give you an overview of all that you do, and also all that you might be doing that is not for you to be do – maybe they belong to someone else in your family or your office. And also what you can pass to someone else to do. If you have children, consider passing domestic chores over to them. It will help them learn responsibility and even appreciate you more.

The thing this list highlights the most is what you are expecting from yourself, and the pressure you might be putting yourself under. The goblins feed off that pressure and like to make it ten times worse with their endless chatter. But relieving yourself of that pressure will also reduce their effect. If you see that list and realise just how much you have been doing, you can be proud of yourself and even feel more accomplished. It will enable you to be more self-forgiving and less tolerant of whatever the goblins have to say.

So give it a go and see how much you are taking on, and then you might find the in-the-moment strategy of the short list more effective, as you slay your chores – and those pesky goblins.

Reconnect

*"Thoughts are the shadows of our feelings
— always darker, emptier and simpler."*
Friedrich Nietzsche

I find the goblins in my head often like to start comparing my life to others, especially my social life – or lack thereof. It likes to question the few friends I have, whether they are good friends, or bad friends, and of course, whether I am a good friend or bad friend if I am not hearing from my friends. It likes to drive me into believing that no one likes me, no one wants to be my friend, and that I am worthless and have no value.

Sound familiar?

This same pattern of thinking could be applied to your work, your family, parenting, any and all aspects of your life.

But when journaling and trying to reframe these thoughts, I uncovered what was actually feeding them. For me, in the instance above, it was loneliness. I felt as though I wasn't connecting with anyone in my life, and no one was connecting with me.

How I combat that in the moment is by deliberately reaching out and connecting with my friends: having a chat, whether online or in person, and arranging a meet up. Reminding myself that we are still friends and there was no truth in what the goblins were telling me.

But the most important point here is not the action I took afterwards of connecting with someone externally, it was realising what was feeding the goblins, and connecting to my true feelings in the moment to resolve the chatter.

Uncovering the real feeling and allowing myself to feel it, without letting the goblins in my head to steer me off the cliff into the land of paranoia and worthless thinking, is what brought them to an end.

Often the negative thoughts in our heads are thrown up as a defensive mechanism against connecting to underlying feelings we don't want to feel. You project these thoughts into your external world picking fault with it, or turn it on yourself, blaming yourself and making yourself wrong – or both.

But if you allow yourself to register the true feeling and just sit with it and experience it, asking yourself, where does it reside in your body? Does it manifest physically? (pain/nausea), acknowledging and accepting that you feel that way, it won't feel as bad, and you will have connected to yourself in the process.

Doing this gives you the opportunity to be compassionate to yourself, highlighting that you are a sensitive being who has needs and maybe they are not being met. Not laying blame anywhere, just knowing it is something you would like to change and maybe turn your mind to changing it – like I did when I reached out and connected with my friends.

So next time you find the goblins singling you out, picking on you and making you wrong in any given situation, ask yourself, what is the real feeling here? What feeling am I avoiding? Lonely, sad, insecure, anxious, unsafe, overwhelmed? And then let yourself feel that true raw feeling and afterwards ask yourself what you need to be able to feel better (whether it is attainable or not).

Remember, none of the feelings are 'wrong', they are YOUR feelings and you're allowed to feel them. And often engaging and connecting to the true raw emotion helps it dissipate. Much like with facing your fears, the thought of it is heavier than the actual experience of it.

Boundaries

Boundaries as a strategy can be difficult to implement as an in-the-moment solution, but they are important to mention because once established it is possible to use them in the moment.

They become effective once you start to recognise the negative internal dialogue and its origins and learn its triggers – the things that spark it into happening.

They are your thoughts, but they are being manipulated by your external world, and then in turn your internal world. Things from the past feed them, but so do things in the present, and it starts turning in a loop, and becomes a noise in your head that just leaves you feeling anxious, overwhelmed or depressed.

Stepping back from whatever feeds the goblins and being able to view it objectively is the first step. And that is where we can start setting boundaries.

Our current world is in turmoil and if you spend a lot of time online like I do, you can't avoid hearing about it. In some ways the noise online feeds the chaos and we get stuck on a merry-go-round, going round and round with it. But that is a choice, and as soon as you understand that, you have the power to say, I'm not going to engage with it, and step off.

You can do this a multitude of ways: switch off your television, switch off your phone, uninstall apps on your phone, use apps to limit your social media use, physically walk away from it, take up a hobby you enjoy. The choices are endless.

I personally never read the news, unless it's a big event or something I want to be informed about. I am kept informed enough by my social media inter-action, which I personally curate. And when I can't, I put my phone down and go and do something else, from cooking, reading a book, binge watching a show, to taking walks in nature and going out with friends.

But your internal dialogue can also be fed by peo-ple, friends and/or family too, it doesn't have to be world events, it can be any social event too. The key is recognising what is triggering it for you and then reducing your engagement with those triggers. That includes stepping away or reducing contact with toxic people whether they are family or friends. An-yone or anything that leaves you feeling upset.

These are physical boundaries and can be hard to implement, so they need to be supported by emotional boundaries – but those can be even harder to implement.

Achieving this comes through self-love, self-respect, self-care, self-compassion and all those other self's which contribute to you considering yourself and putting yourself front and centre, not just in your life but in your mind.

And this is not a selfish act – let's get that clear right here. It is not selfish in any way to consider yourself, care about yourself, or want your life to be full of the things that make you happy. Those that claim it is are the people that have given their lives over to someone or something else, who no longer have control in their lives or take responsibility for the way they think or behave. Some of those people believe you have to suffer in life for it to have meaning, or unless you are serving someone or something bigger than you, your life has no purpose. They have given their personal power over to someone or something else.

Taking control of your thinking and not allowing negatives voices to run your life, means taking back your personal power, particularly in the area of choice.

Choosing to change your thinking and care about your mental health is the first step. For some, that alone is a boundary, saying no to those that are expecting them to say yes.

And to do that you have to start with how you feel.

Tune in and dare to feel.

As I talked about in the 'Reconnect' chapter, you can't know yourself unless you actually feel your feelings. And the only way to do that is by listening to how you feel, and sitting with it, and letting it consume you (however hard that is).

Once you have learnt how you feel, which you can do on a daily basis by asking yourself how you feel – literally ask yourself every day – and listen to the response, mentally and physically, then you can start to trust your feelings ... because you know how you feel.

And with trust comes self-assurance (another one of those self's I was talking about), which means you can feel secure in how you feel because you know how you feel.

And from there you grow self-trust, self-confidence and all the other self's that increase your strength and ability to face the world and combat the goblins in your mind.

But just to clarify, listening to your feelings is actually what self-love, self-compassion and self-care looks like. It's considering yourself and your feelings.

From that point you can start to set emotional boundaries based on those feelings, like: 'I don't feel like doing that today', or 'that isn't something I want to do', and feel okay saying no to doing it (you can apply this to any and all things, from housework to going to family events).

Or on the positive side: 'I feel like doing that today', 'that's something I've always wanted to do', and saying yes to something that you enjoy.

Because how you feel matters to you. Not anyone else at this stage, just you.

I used to look at my garden and think, why should I do it, no one appreciates it, who cares if it is a mess? Why do I want to put all that energy into something no one cares about? And then I realised: I cared; I was the one who appreciated it when it looked nice. So I started doing it for myself, no one else. And it made me happy.

Once you feel confident putting your feelings first internally (by checking in with how you feel), you will start to feel stronger doing that externally. Saying no to things you don't want and saying yes to things you do want when it comes to socialising, work-life, and family interaction.

Boundaries may only start with little things like switching off the news, reducing your time on social media – or muting/blocking/curating what you see on social media. But once you start committing to them you will feel more confident and trust yourself to set bigger more meaningful boundaries.

It will give you a strong sense of self, and you will feel like you have more power to make decisions and commit to them, as well as follow through and rely on yourself.

Resist Resistance

"What resists, persists."
Chris Witceki

Resisting resistance is a bit of a mouthful, but I don't really like using the word 'surrender' because that sounds like giving up or giving in and that is not what this strategy is about at all. I could use the word 'acceptance' but that's not what this strategy is about either, because accepting negative internal dialogue is exactly the opposite of what I am trying to help you do.

However, resisting negative internal dialogue can look like many things:

1) arguing with the goblins, which often ends up with you going round in circles.

2) trying to block out their chatter by self medicating with alcohol, or drugs.

3) contemplating death (suicidal ideation).

That last is pretty harsh and might be shocking, but I get the feeling that if you have picked up this book to try and find some help with the negative voices in your head, you might have come across it at some point. And if you ARE reading this, it means that you are actively trying to find solutions other than that, so let's try and do that.

So what does NOT resisting look like?

Resisting resistance looks like refusing to engage with the voices. You are aware they are there; you can hear their chatter, but you don't act on it.

You don't try and argue, you don't try and reason, you don't try and rationalise whatever they are saying. You literally let them run like film credits through your mind. You observe them, and you literally let them go.

You'd be surprised how powerful that makes you and how quickly it reduces them.

I don't mean listen to them, just know they are there and that the words aren't real. They are borne of a multitude of other things none of which are real, and are just reflections or memories being thrown up by the subconscious, like an echo chamber.

So this strategy is acceptance in that you accept that interacting, engaging or resisting them is futile. (Yes, in some way like the Borg, but the collective will not overrule the one in this instance – if you haven't watched Star Trek, this might go over your head, and that's okay).

And this strategy is also surrendering to their noise by not actively stopping them. You can go about your day and do other things, distract yourself if you like, but not in an active way to deliberately block them.

In that respect you could say this is an easy strategy, but it can be hard to ignore them and go about your day, and it may feel like you are failing in your efforts to stop them, but you are not. You are not allowing them to disrupt your life and feel bad. Like when a bully is trying to put you down, but you don't really care enough about what the bully is saying for it to affect you, so their words have no impact.

And yes, the negative voices in your head are bullies; the goblin analogy represents the voices in your head as someone wanting to belittle and humiliate you. But that voice isn't real, there is no person inside your head, there are only fragments of conversations that have hurt you, and negative beliefs about yourself that have grown from them. And due to overwhelm or stress in your life they are now playing on a loop at any given moment.

And this soundtrack might be stuck on repeat, but this strategy involves you letting it play in the background like white noise or elevator muzak that isn't pleasant but you can ignore and tolerate.

Talk To Someone

*"Everything becomes a little different as soon as
it is spoken out loud."*
Hermann Hesse

As an in-the-moment strategy talking to someone might not be so easy. It depends who is in your life and if you have a trusted person to talk to about whatever is going on in your head.

It isn't always easy to tell others how you feel, especially if you feel they will view you as someone who is complaining about life. I've had that happen a lot. I am very open and happy to talk on many topics, often expressing whatever I am struggling with in my life and things that affect me from my past. Some of the people in my life, who I had thought of as friends, couldn't handle it, and I've had a lot of people move away from me in my friend circles. It hasn't been easy, but I've learnt about boundaries, and deciding who are the right people to share my life problems with and who aren't.

Fortunately I've had a couple of people who I could turn to and a community of friends on social media where I can express those things. It's helped to have people to reach out to, who then reassure me that I am not alone and sympathise with me. It might not make it all better, but it helps me say things out loud.

Even if it is just admitting to someone that you're having a bad day and talking about how you honestly feel, either in real life or on social media (under an anonymous name if it feels safer), saying it out loud can help.

Hearing the words outside yourself gives them another perspective, plus being honest about how you feel, and more importantly, identifying how you feel, can make a huge difference.

Expressing your feelings, whatever they are: sad, lonely, angry, frustrated, hurt, disappointed, ashamed, and so on, can really help process those feelings more easily.

Bottling them up and pushing them down often only makes them last longer and become bigger, especially in the mind. And the goblins are particularly adept at growing those little sensitive molehills into huge painful mountains.

The sooner you find a way to express it in a safe way, the better.

I'm also an advocate of talk therapy. I've been in therapy on three occasions: twice in my early 20s, where I was initially helped with dealing with panic attacks and processing past trauma, and again in my late 30s, after a breakdown. I spent six years in therapy with a 'Mindfulness' psychologist.

Therapy is certainly not an in-the-moment strategy, but it is a safe place to talk to someone, and worth considering if you don't feel like you are progressing with finding ways to deal with the noise in your head.

The first step is recognising you need help, and the second is daring to actually seek help through your doctor or finding out who's in your local area. But depending on what country you live in and your income, whether you can actually get the help you need is a different matter.*

So in the meantime, consider who you could talk to in your life, either on the phone or in person. You could even send a private message or an email to a friend online, just to get something off your chest, or a particular thought that is spinning round your head. Alternatively, you can put it on social media, and let others know you could do with a kind word, or some reassurance.

Daring to speak out is an act of courage as well as an act of self-care. Standing up and admitting that things aren't perfect and you need help is a way of supporting yourself and advocating for yourself. Pushing through the fear and admitting it to yourself and to someone else is the first step to making it better.

*I talk more about therapy in the second part of this book.

Worst Case Scenario

"If you train worst case scenarios consistently, they will no longer be worst case scenarios."
Rener Gracie

A great deal of goblin chatter is based off fear and anxiety. It usually starts with everyday things which then escalate into catastrophic events. We all know how that goes, but how I have tackled this in my own mind is by actually starting with the worst case scenario – sort of call their bluff.

I used to suffer panic attacks on a nightly basis, and they centred around a fear of throwing up. I would have my dinner, feel full up, then my mind would start scaring me by telling me I felt sick and I might be sick, and wouldn't it be awful if I was sick and couldn't stop being sick. It was a post traumatic stress response after suffering a nasty bout of food poisoning a year or so before. In the midst of my panic I would shake and sweat and pace. But the one way I could tell whether it was fake or not, whether I was actually feeling sick or it was panic induced, was by going straight to the thought: 'Okay then, if we're going to be sick, let's be sick.' And immediately the sensation of feeling sick would disappear.

In most cases, fear is False Evidence Appearing Real, and I've found the best way to dispel it is by turning into it.

So when I am worrying about something and the goblins kick in, I go okay, then, what is the worst case scenario in this instance? Would I go to prison? Would I die? Would I be hospitalised? Would I be homeless? What would actually happen? What is the reality? And I work my way from that point back to what is realistic and that makes me feel better.

It *could* work out that you scare yourself more, so I would recommend trying this for the first time with something small, like, 'What will happen if I don't go to the gym today?' or with someone helping you – close friend or family member – just so you don't go off the deep end and they are there to throw you a lifeline and bring you back to shore.

Talking of water, when my son was six years old he learnt at school about a huge flood that had happened in the country in the 1950s where over two thousand people lost their lives. Afterwards, every evening at bedtime he would worry it would flood, especially if it was raining. This went on for weeks, and despite all my reassurances that it wouldn't happen he still worried about it. So one night I asked him, 'Okay, so what would we do if it DID flood?'

And we talked through all the possibilities and the likely scenarios. It made him feel better thinking through all the potential outcomes, as though he had a sort of contingency plan. He had a realistic idea of what might happen, and felt reassured that he could cope with it.

And that is what you need to do if you find yourself in this situation, with your mind blowing up the slightest worry into something disastrous. Don't be afraid to ask yourself, what is the worst that can happen? and work your way back to the actual reality. As an adult you are far more likely to have a realistic view of that reality than a six year old, and if not, far more capable of finding out.

I have found it helps to equip myself for every eventuality, if only to put my negative internal dialogue in its place – which means shut it up, the aim of this strategy.

Wallow

Yes, you read the chapter title right, wallow is indeed the strategy I'm recommending. Give yourself a break and have a day off from life. Let yourself feel things you might not be letting yourself feel.

Sometimes I'm busy holding off expressing sadness or upset because I'm too busy writing, running a household, managing two children and I just don't 'have time' to process how I am feeling. But self care is all about making time for yourself, whatever method that is for you.

It can look like anything from lying in bed all day, sitting in front of the telly and binge watching your favourite show, or having a really good cry! It can also include exercising, meditating, reading, journaling, going for a walk. There are no rules – which is the point. You do whatever you feel like and let everything else drop for the day, because there's always tomorrow.

Most people spend a lot of time putting on a public face and holding it in place, but there's nothing wrong with having a day or two without having to wear it. Just let yourself be and relax, no judgement, no expectations. Be compassionate with yourself. Be kind; talk to yourself as you would a child in need of love and reassurance. Be comforting and nurturing; listen to your needs and your feelings and give caring responses to them.

You may have heard of the 'mindfulness' concept, or the 'being present' concept, (and I'm calling these 'in-the-moment' strategies), all of which relate to being here now, in this moment, doing what YOU need to do to feel better and get the noise in your head to abate, if only for a few hours or a day, and that includes wallowing.

And what I mean by that is actually let it all go, not sitting there letting the goblins eat up your mind – and your free time – by telling you, you're a bad person for taking time out for yourself. Give yourself a chance to feel any of the emotions you have had pent up. Let out whatever might be behind those nasty voices in your head: disappointment, anger, hurt, sadness, loneliness, frustration. Express them in whatever way you want (as long as it is not by hurting anyone else – including you).

Giving yourself a down day, or several down days, is healthy. It is a misconception that people are happy all the time no matter how they might appear at work, or school, or on social media. Being human is to feel, and sometimes those feelings aren't going to be great feelings. And to process those feelings you have to allow yourself to feel them, and if that takes the form of having a good wallow, so be it.

The essence of the word wallow means to 'indulge' oneself, 'to roll oneself about in a lazy, relaxed, or ungainly manner' – so do that, allow yourself that time. But as always the point is to reduce the negative chatter in your mind and not increase it.

Allowing yourself to feel may seem scary, you may be worried about letting go. You may think you will be overwhelmed with your feelings and not be able to control them and end up in that state forever. But I can assure you, having had days where I've let myself cry all day, there is always an end. There is always a time when you are all cried out. And yes, you might feel a bit empty afterwards, and numb. It expends a lot of energy. But that doesn't mean that you won't come back to yourself. In fact you're more likely to come back with more energy and vigour, because (hopefully) it won't be accompanied by the incessant negative chatter.

Whatever you choose to do, make sure you are the number one priority.

Overused but are they overrated?

Meditation

"Meditation is not a way of making your mind quiet. It's a way of entering into the quiet that's already there — buried under the 50,000 thoughts the average person thinks every day."
Deepak Chopra

The saying goes that Buddha said you should meditate at least 20 minutes a day, unless you have a busy mind, then you should meditate for an hour a day. For most of us that just isn't realistic.

There are a wealth of articles on websites, and YouTube videos about meditating. It's a huge industry that includes clothing, courses, and retreats. Personally I'd love to go on a retreat, but I wonder how successful I would be at it, because I tend to meditate randomly, when I feel the need and usually I seem to snap out of it after 10 minutes and can't get my head back into it. That's normal. People with busy minds struggle with it.

But is it overrated? Especially as an in-the-moment strategy? My answer is: no.

The aim here is to find a way to reduce and/or stop the negative internal dialogue going on in your mind on a day-to-day basis, and even if you only achieve this for a couple of minutes, it's an achievement.

The practice of meditation is about pulling back the veil of noise in the mind and finding the calm behind it, and becoming aware that it is possible to achieve that calm.

Once you get a glimpse of it, you can find ways to increase its accessibility, which won't just bring about mental calm but often a physical calm as the two work as one, you can't separate mind from body – even though Western culture likes to treat them as separate things.

And although meditation is touted as a daily event that needs to happen in a particular place, for a length of time, and treated as some special sacred ritual, it doesn't have to be that way.

Have you heard of one-minute meditation? It involves pausing in whatever you're doing, wherever you are and literally just taking a breath. You focus on your breathing for a minute, disconnecting from the chatter in your head, as though pulling the plug to reset it just for a moment.

You don't have to be in a specially designated room, or dressed any particular way, or take specific time out to do it, you literally just hit pause for a minute. You can be in your car driving, at work, or in the midst of cooking the family meal – anywhere.

As soon as you feel the need to clear you mind, just think about your breathing: count two while inhaling, then four when (slowly) exhaling, then hold for a count of two (neither inhale or exhale), and begin again. Consciously feel your body, from top to toe, and physically relax – even tensing each part of the body and consciously relaxing it.

And that's it. A one minute meditation.

If you want to keep going you might find thoughts coming into your mind. And if you find yourself engaging with them, the moment you realise you are, return your mind to your breathing. Feel the breath going in through the nose and out through the mouth. And like I said in the chapter, Resist Resistance, imagine your thoughts running like the credits of a movie in the back of your mind. Don't engage with them. Just leave them.

But if it is not for you and you struggle with it, leave it. It's not for everyone and that's okay. There is nothing wrong with you, you haven't failed, it's just not what will work for you to rid yourself of your chattering goblins.

Exercise

"I have to exercise in the morning before my brain figures out what I'm doing."

The quote above isn't attributed to anyone, it's listed as a gym joke, but there is a lot of truth in it. Sometimes it's more stressful thinking about doing exercise than it is to just get on with it. I have found that if I think it through first, I feel like I have already done it, so instead I choose to just get on with it — and if I don't do it early, I rarely get to it at all.

Exercise is lauded everywhere across the world, online and offline, as something we should all be doing. Jogging, running, playing sport, going to the gym — it's everywhere. I will confess that I have yet to ever step inside a gym (outside of a school gym that is), a fact I'm actually quite proud of. I tell people I prefer not to exercise in public. In truth, I fear that it will increase the goblins ever insistent chatter about comparing me to everyone.

However, as I am now in my fifties, I have certain parts of my body that are weakening or have been injured, and I have to do a certain amount of exercise. I do a mixture of physio exercises, yoga and pilates, and I do find them helpful, not just to keep me mobile and supple, but as a means to take mental time out.

So is exercise overrated? Especially as an in-the-moment strategy to get the goblins in our head to shut up? My answer is: no.

I don't mean in terms of just deciding when the noise is too much, to set off jogging round the block – although you can, no one is stopping you, but in terms of making a simple movement at that time. Even just changing your posture will actually alter your mental state and perception, because it affects how we think and view the world.

How we carry our body and move about has a combined physical and neurological effect on the thought processes in our brain. I first read about this in a Tony Robbins book called, Unlimited Power. He talked about depression and how it is a physical state as much as a mental one. I have since read multiple articles about how our posture not only affects our confidence, but how we relate to others and the world.

So exercise in any form is worth considering, and as a strategy, you can choose to get up (or even remain seated) and stretch at any given moment. Literally stretch and look up – even if it is at your ceiling, and take a deep breath. Connect with yourself and your body in that moment.

I also found that once I started doing my exercises on a regular, defined basis (for me that's three times a week for about 15-20 minutes, a routine I worked out for myself), I found it easier to maintain. And the consistency and persistence has helped my body feel a lot better, and in turn, made me feel better.

Knowing I can follow through and commit to it has confirmed I can do that in other areas of my life too, even if they are only small and incremental. It helps me keep sight of my goals and take action on them every day, because I can tell the goblins that I CAN do it, that it's just a matter of building on what I have already achieved.

And that is the point with all of these strategies, knowing that you can do something, no matter how small every day to improve the state of your mind.

Walking in nature

*"In every walk with nature, one receives far more
than he seeks."*
John Muir

Is walking in nature any different from exercise? It
is a form of exercise, yes, but a lot of exercise takes
place indoors, and even though running or jogging
may include being in nature, the focus isn't always
on the location.

There are again, countless articles promoting the
mental health benefits of taking walks in nature,
even scientific proof about how it reduces stress
hormones in your blood. They can't be missed if you
spend any amount of time online looking at anything
in the mental health arena.

Reconnecting with yourself, creating mental head
space as you walk about embracing, enjoying and
looking at nature; all of this can help reduce the flow

of negative internal dialogue, and general chatter in your head in general – especially if you don't wish to partake on your own.

But is doing this overrated? No.

And is it possible for it to be an in-the-moment strategy? My answer is: yes.

I know it isn't always easy to get into nature, and to do so fully you may need to travel. Not all of us are blessed with living in rural areas where there is a lot of greenage. Being able to access nature is not always cost or time effective, especially if you do work full time, whether day work or night work. But the sky is also part of the nature, and even if it only involves looking up into the sky and taking a second to appreciate it, that is an in-the-moment strategy.

Mentally stepping out of all your noisy thoughts and taking that time to see it and recognise it. You can do the same with a tree, shrub or flowers, whether in other people's gardens or even balcony boxes, or along a main road. Looking at it, acknowledging it, and pondering on its beauty or marvelling at its growth is how this would work in the moment.

Even within your office, if you have a window you can look out and catch a glimpse of the sky or clouds, or even a tree across the street, the principle is still the same, moving yourself out of a mindset where negative thoughts can dominate.

It might not be the full 'walking in nature'; maybe it is just 'seeing nature' but it is essentially the same idea and has the same effect on your mind. It gives you a chance to take a break. Even at night, there can be things to see and appreciate, even on a cloudy night. Try and notice them, because doing so will distract you from whatever is going on in your head.

The walking part, however, is significant and worth considering if you can make the time. Walking is known as a good way to 'reset the brain' because the action itself means that a large part of your brain is busy with the processes required for moving your body and breathing, especially after twenty minutes or so. And if you are in an anxious state of mind walking uses up the excess adrenaline it creates.

It is very much where the physical and mental processes of our bodies are linked. Strolling will affect our mood and the tone of our inner dialogue as it responds to the motion of our body. Walking quickly or more relaxed also has an effect. But walking doesn't require as much effort as running and jogging so we are also able to open our minds to other, more helpful thoughts, and maybe identify patterns and come up with solutions through such walks.

And the nature part enables us to keep our minds on our surroundings, changing the dialogue into one of enjoyment and wonder. Thereby if you are city or town living, and not able to get into nature easily, it can make it harder.

Walking the streets doesn't quite have the same effect if it is crowded and full of the noise of other people. It's like adding more voices to those in your head, and you're more likely to experience something that will irritate and frustrate you and potentially increase them further, providing openings for more goblins to show up and wreak their destruction. So consider where you go for your walk as much as the walk itself, even if it is a tiny park close to your work where you can sit for a few minutes observing the plants or wildlife.

But either way, this strategy is one where just taking a moment to observe nature can help distract from the negative dialogue and bring you joy, even if it is only a moment.

Affirmations

An affirmation is one of those buzz words that swept through the personal development world and into meme form on social media and people started to view as negative. (I talk about 'toxic positivity' in a separate chapter). I've been told by many people they are harmful, but a lot of people don't fully understand, 1) what they are, and 2) their function.

Affirmations are words, sentences and phrases you repeat to yourself on a daily basis. They are words or sentences that have meaning for you. Through the repetition of the word or phrase you can train your mind to provide a healthier internal dialogue.

At the beginning of this book I talk about retraining your thinking. I talk about what feeds the conscious mind, and how it runs in an endless loop with the subconscious, until you break the conscious stream and literally replace the thoughts and words. And to do this persistently, because one day your subconscious will start throwing up those replacement thoughts and words automatically.

Affirmations do that; they are replacement thoughts and words that help you retrain and reframe your thoughts. That is their purpose and that is why you should choose them personally and not randomly. Like with anything, only take what resonates with you and leave the rest. What suits another person might not suit you.

Do I consider them overused? In some cases people become completely obsessive in their use of them, especially online.

But are they overrated to combat negative internal dialogue? My answer is: no.

They fit an in-the-moment strategy well; if you find the goblins in your mind running rampant and telling you things about yourself which are not true and are hurtful, you can repeat a word or phrase in response to combat them. But do be discerning in the words you choose for yourself. Believing in what you say is paramount, or knowing that deep down it is true, even if you struggle to believe it in the first place.

For example, in my early twenties, I struggled to see my value and always put other people before me, I believed I was not important or significant in any way. It made me depressed and anxious. My therapist gave me the task of coming up with a sentence to repeat to myself to shift this belief. The sentence I came up with was: 'It's my life and I'm the most important person in it.' It took me a long time (three years) to honestly believe it, but it made a difference every time I said it. I would particularly call on it in times of struggle – and still do.

There are less emphatic phrases which are helpful to stop your mind going off on a tangent about things too. I have also adopted the 'Not my monkey, not my circus', when I find myself being triggered by drama or events in someone else's life.

They don't have to be something deep and meaningful – but they can be. They can be whatever makes sense to you and helps you in your day.

A word about gaslighting.

People are using this term everywhere at the moment, and I came across someone using this term on themselves, saying that they had 'gaslit' themselves. What they mean by that is that they were lying to themselves. And some people believe that affirmations do that; that you are lying to yourself when you are repeating something to yourself that you don't actually believe.

What a person believes informs every aspect of their lives, but you can change what you believe, especially about yourself – both good and bad. A lot of negative internal dialogue is created by someone telling you, you are bad or wrong in some way (physically or in your personality), and you actually accepted it and internalised it, resulting in you believing it, even though it's not actually true.

The point of affirmations is to change that. You 'affirm' something good about yourself. It is not a lie to believe something positive about yourself. In fact, it has been found that to cancel out one bad thing said to you, you need at least ten or more positive things.

We have been conditioned by society not to believe the good, because it's claimed that it will lead us to think we are better than others. But that simply isn't true. Knowing you are a worthy human being is a necessary part of having any kind of confidence and being able to push forward in life and achieve the things you want to achieve. Don't be persuaded to believe otherwise.

So, if there are words or phrases that you find helpful to soothe you and quiet the noise in your head, don't be afraid to use them. We need every tool in our box in keep the pesky goblins in their place, or drive them off for good!

Potentially Harmful strategies

Demonising a part of yourself

"You have been criticising yourself for years, and it hasn't worked. Try approving of yourself and see what happens."
Louise Hay

A lot of people who find their negative internal dialogue overwhelming separate it off by demonising it. They give it an identity, like a separate part of themselves, and hate upon it, referring to it as a bully or a nasty part of themselves they don't like. They might give it a name, and whenever they hear this voice in their head, blame it for all the hurt it is inflicting.

The premise of this idea as a way to deal with the negative chatter is removing yourself from it, taking a step back and seeing it as something that isn't a part of you so you can shut it off, or pretend it is not you, to try and shut it down. And it might work for a while, but ultimately, it's just playing a game with your own mind, and not resolving the underlying issue, which is about accepting all elements of your-self, no matter how dark and painful.

When I was suffering intense paranoid thoughts during my breakdown, thoughts about how others didn't like me and didn't want to be around me and how it wasn't a surprise because I had done this, that and the other to upset them, and it was all my fault, I called this voice the paranoid monster. And in my mind I saw it as a separate part of me, one I would imagine shutting in a wardrobe to get it to shut up. I referred to that element of myself as something sep-arate to me, like I had turned into someone else when it turned up in my head. But I hadn't.

Through therapy it was revealed to me that it was actually my inner child (the child part of ourselves that lives inside each and every one of us), who was scared and frightened and needed comfort and sup-port, and I was doing to it what my single parent had done to me: shut me out and ignore me. It was very powerful when I realised this. I sat in my car after-wards crying.

Not feeling compassion for this part of myself was what made it continue to come up. The ward-robe would burst open and the next time the para-noid monster would be even more hysterical and turn me into the person I really didn't like being, one who got upset, angry, frustrated and turn into some-one who sounded a lot like my single parent when they had been screaming at me in my teenage. It would wipe me out, drain me of all my energy – and worst of all it caused others to move away from me and leave me isolated and alone.

Pushing away the elements of ourselves that are scary, hurt or painful, doesn't work as a strategy to resolve the presence of goblins in your head in the long term. Learning to understand what is feeding them does, along with being sympathetic, gentle and nurturing to yourself when they are running amok.

Recovering a peaceful mind and finding a balance to keep it that way encompasses being kind, and forgiving to yourself. Knowing when to cut yourself some slack and not constantly criticise yourself.

So if you have already created a separate identity for those nasty voices, maybe invite them to tea and have a chat and find out exactly what part of you they are, and why they are saying those things. It's a part of you, and you need to become friends with it to support all of you.

Dissociate

"At times I seek dissociation to associate with myself."
Booma Balan

To dissociate is a psychological term that describes what some people do in response to traumatic external events. They disconnect from themselves and drift off mentally to another place, so they don't have to think or feel or accept what is happening around them. When some people get overwhelmed with the noise in their head they do this too.

In simple terms it is known as daydreaming or fantasising, but generally it means not being present or engaging with anything or anyone around you. It's considered an unhelpful way to deal with what is going on, even though for those being abused it develops as a survival mechanism.

For me it very much kept me alive throughout my teen years. I developed a very elaborate and detailed world I would skip into, where I was another version of me living a completely different life, in a different country, with lots of loving people around me, where I was highly successful. But in later years, when I found myself in difficult situations it kept me disengaged and disconnected from my family and friends.

During my therapy I would sort of listen into myself during these visits and work out what it was I was seeking in this fantasy world, so I could work out what I needed in my real world to bring me back and keep me present.

I realised I was self-soothing through imagined people giving me approval. I worked out that I was the one who could give me the approval and comfort I sought, and over time and with a lot of work reduced the instances of it.

As a strategy to deal with a lot of mental stress and noise in the head, it can be effective, but in the long term it has negative consequences. I didn't form friendships or healthy connections in the real world, and I would be distracted and neglectful of those I did have around me, withdrawing or walking away from them.

So although it's nice to skip off to a fantasy in your mind, it's not healthy and doesn't help you create an enjoyable life in your reality.

Toxic Positivity

"We cannot selectively numb emotions, when we numb the painful emotions, we also numb the positive emotions."
Brené Brown

Toxic positivity is a term that came about in response to the explosion on the internet and social media of memes and articles shared by people encouraging others to maintain a positive outlook at all costs, even when they're struggling, claiming that it only takes a positive mindset to become happy.

During this time it was considered wrong to express anything online that could be construed as negative, like if you didn't like something, or something awful had happened to you, or you were just having a bad day. It meant people developed masking (putting on a face for others), and felt pressured to pretend their lives were great when in reality they might be falling apart.

Now the tables have turned, and people expressing these positive sentiments about being grateful and looking on the bright side of things are rejected among the majority of people, and sharing these kinds of things is considered toxic positivity.

I myself experienced this when a social group I set up to find others who had settled in the country I was living in, turned on me because they thought talking about the struggles I had with the culture shouldn't be expressed. They had no interest in talking about them or sharing their own, only in shutting me down and pushing me away – and out of the group entirely as it turned out. It no longer became a place where people could find empathy or solace when they realised they weren't alone with things they found different, which had been my intention. It became a clique of people who were only interested in what I call surface chatter, about children, work, cooking, and holidays.

In our society we are taught not to express our emotions from a very young age. We are told anger is bad and being happy all the time is good. We are told not to be scared, not to feel anxious and not to feel sad. This means when we do experience these emotions, we don't know how to process them or what to do with them, and end up pushing them down or away.

But bad feelings left unfelt or unprocessed will build up and become overwhelming, and trigger other problems like depression, anxiety, paranoia and other more extreme mental health problems like self harming and compulsive disorders.

We all have our dark sides; we can feel angry and negative about things and sometimes aren't always feeling in a kind mood. That is allowed. You are allowed those feelings.

I've never been someone who pretends to be happy and jolly for the sake of it, often because I rarely am unless I'm in the right company. But I have learnt to be silent with people I know won't be interested or understanding, or simply withdraw from them.

With everything there is a balance. It is okay to feel good and be happy and share that when you are, just as you can also express when you are having a bad day. It's a matter of not suppressing your real feelings and being yourself, and feeling comfortable sharing it.

Part Two

What is feeding the Goblins?

Introduction to Part Two

In-the-moment strategies are helpful on a day-to-day basis, but sometimes we need to look behind the curtain, like Dorothy did in the land of Oz, to find out what is actually causing our minds to become a playground for the goblins who like to taunt us with their lies and make us believe and relive the worst about ourselves.

In this section I outline some of the things that are behind a noisy mind, and the process I went through to reach a quieter mind.

This is for your own contemplation. Some of it may not apply, but take what resonates and leave the rest.

Remember, it is all about you and all down to you. You have the power to change it – we all do.

Why the voices in your head?

"You can't calm the storm, so stop trying. What you can do is calm yourself. The storm will pass."
Timber Hawkeye

When you ask someone why they have what I call a 'noisy head' you'll receive an array of answers: stress, overwork, overwhelm, anxiety, trauma. However, the majority of them won't have delved into exactly how their head got that way, or whose voices actually belong to the negative chatter they are subjected to every day. They're too busy struggling to deal with it. But it's only when we look at what started it that we can really start to resolve it on a more permanent basis.

As babies & young children we look to our parents to learn about who we are and how to be. We look to them for reassurance and comfort. Through the situations they provide, we learn how to generate our confidence, our happiness to become whole people. When that is disrupted the process doesn't work. There can be many things that will disrupt it: parental abuse, bullying at school, a traumatic event – or a series of them, even having a sensitive disposition. Any and all of these things can fundamentally undermine someone's self-esteem in life; their ability to be secure in themselves and create a life where they are happy and doing the things they want to be doing.

The voices in your head belong to the people or events that have hurt you. When someone has berated you or made you feel bad, or something has happened to make you feel ashamed, you have repeated those voices and added on to them throughout your life, continuing to punish and berate yourself.

That sounds blunt but it's the truth, and we need to reach the truth when the voices in our heads are telling us lies – and they are, have no doubt about that.

Here's an example from my own childhood:

When I was nine years old, I was on a train with my siblings and my mother. It was a period of turmoil; my mother had split up with my stepfather, and we had moved away, but every weekend we would return to what had been the family home to pack up our belongings. This particular Friday while traveling back to our family home, my mother told us that we wouldn't be going there, that on Tuesday my stepfather had come and emptied the house and a friend of hers, who had been feeding the cats for us, had only managed to retrieve about a third of our belongings. That in itself was traumatic enough, but when I asked why she hadn't said anything to us earlier in the week, she had snapped, "Because you talk too much and can't keep your mouth shut! You'd tell everyone!" It was so vicious and unexpected it cut me to the core.

And from that moment on I became scared of talking too much, and that I wasn't trustworthy. Even now, over forty years on, when I am out with friends or on the phone with a friend, I come away wondering if I said too much. The nasty goblins in my head telling me that people don't like me because of it. And it caused me to neither trust myself or trust people, which has made it difficult for me to form friendships and relationships.

Even now, writing this, there's a whisper of a voice in my head saying, 'and people have confirmed you talk too much, are not to be trusted and that they don't like you.' And I can't argue with that, because when you are someone who isn't sure of yourself, you overcompensate, and in my case that meant I talked too much and overshared, especially when nervous, and it hasn't always been received well by others.

There are many other moments for me personally that have also contributed to this noise. I was bullied at school. I remember someone pulling me aside once and telling me that if I changed myself I might have more friends. I'm not quite sure what those changes were expected to be, but it was again a clear sign that I wasn't accepted by them, which added to the voices.

And then even in my late thirties, when I founded and ran a social group, I ended up having a breakdown due to the voices escalating into extreme paranoia every time I was in the company of the other members, triggered by nasty comments from a few who wanted me excluded. I ended up excluding myself for years instead.

Not pleasant times, but it enabled me to seek the help I needed and rebuild, and understand my inherent value, and return my personal power.

Having been raised by a single parent who taught me that other people's opinions of me matter more than I did (because that is what they believed), it's been hard to believe I am as worthy as the next person, and that I'm only punishing myself believing otherwise.

And what it comes down to in the end is how you feel about yourself.

If you don't feel worthy, valuable, and enough, insecurities take over and negative internal dialogue blossoms, taking on the voices of the people who have said the things that have hurt you, or that you are particularly sensitive to.

We spend a lot of time looking for validation externally, but the truth is we need to validate ourselves internally. We need to befriend ourselves and start talking and listening to ourselves in a different way.

No, it's not easy, it takes work, continuous, persistent work. But it IS possible. So where do you begin?

Meeting yourself where you are

*"Not one drop of my self-worth depends on your
acceptance of me."*
Quincy Jones

Not feeling worthy, enough, or valuable, or not believing in yourself, your talents, or your ability to accomplish your dreams, manifests itself in many ways, including self-doubt, procrastination and self-sabotage. And this is what feeds the goblins, those negative voices which result in you feeling bad about anything you are attempting to achieve, and often giving up on it.

To change those voices means to change those feelings, which are based in beliefs about yourself. And although it's worth uncovering the roots of those beliefs, it's not necessary when starting to change how you feel about yourself on a daily basis.

And yes, it is possible to change how you feel about yourself, because I've done it. It just takes persistence.

People talk about self-approval and self-acceptance (all those 'selfs' again), but it's not possible to suddenly start feeling those things, or start 'doing' those things. You can't just switch it on like a light. You may even think you DO actively approve and accept yourself – and maybe you do in some areas.

But there is a process which I uncovered through my work on myself and my time in therapy that helped me understand how to become self-approved and self-accepting, and in particular, believe in myself and my inherent value and to feel better about myself. Those were the things that reduced the negative chatter in my head and stopped the goblins being able to take control.

(Be aware that this is the process that worked for me, it may not be identical to what you need. You may need to tweak it or alter it to fit where you are in your life, or match the reason why you picked up this book. Take what works for you and leave the rest. Be inspired to find your own process and your own truth. But use this as an example.)

When I began, I realised that the key thing I was missing was self-trust. I didn't trust myself to do what needed to be done, from small things to big things. I didn't trust myself to follow-through, be persistent or consistent. I didn't trust myself to be supportive of me and not to let me down.

Trust and believing in yourself walk hand in hand. If you don't trust yourself, you won't believe in yourself.

So how do you trust yourself?

You trust yourself by listening to yourself.

I don't mean to the constant chatter of negative thoughts in your head, obviously. They only provide more questions than answers, based on biased 'evidence' – evidence collected from the outside world that you believe proves the negative voices are right. No, I mean listening to your heart, to your soul, to the very essence of who you are inside.

To do that you need to sit quietly and reach out with your conscious mind to your body, feeling every part of it and settling on the heart. And then asking it how it feels about the things you are struggling with – yes, I mean literally ask it, either out loud or in your head, and feel the physical response your body gives.

I know this sounds weird, but feelings are a physical thing. You feel bad when you are sick to your stomach, tense your muscles, or feel tired; and you feel good by the opposite: a spark of excitement in your stomach, relaxing your muscles, or feeling energised.

Listening to your heart means tuning into your body, and its response. It is how you connect to yourself. You trust what you know, and if you know how you feel about something, you can trust it.

However, it doesn't stop you second guessing, or doubting those feelings. The trick to breaking that mental cycle is a simple one: Action.

If you take action based on your true feelings you start building something that is past the questioning stage, something tangible. You are supporting your feelings by doing something. You are following through and creating a previous record to refer to – real evidence!

And the more times you do that – take action based off your true feelings – the more you will trust both your feelings and yourself. It supports belief in your feelings and creates trust for the next time and then the next, building a rapport with yourself, a history, and a connection.

These actions can look like something you want to do or something you don't want to do; saying yes to something or saying no to it. It can be something simple like deciding you want to create a routine or habit that is better for you and actively doing it every day.

For instance, I set up a work-out routine where I work out for twenty minutes three times a week, and rather than allow it to drop off and stop after a month or two, which is what I used to do, I have maintained it for going on two years now. I remind myself that I am committing to this for me, not for anyone else. I shift days occasionally to suit, but I have remained consistent and persist in following through with it.

I feel stronger, not just physically but emotionally and mentally. I am proud of myself. I have created a history with myself where I have followed through and maintained something I want.

When doing this make sure it is something you can actively achieve; start small, not big.

If you have a big goal, try and break it down into small steps, thinking about what action you can take on a daily basis to work towards it. Like going to bed half an hour earlier every night. I did that to give me time to read because I wanted to make it a priority, because I needed to research information for something I wanted to write. I also started leaving my phone downstairs so I didn't end up endlessly scrolling on social media.

They aren't big things, but they are things that support me and my well-being. Things that I follow through on a daily basis that build up that trust.

Doing these things isn't easy; you have to believe you are worth it, and take the time for you to start and maintain this process.

If you honestly want to change how you feel, you have to make time for you and your feelings.

You have to get to a point where you ask yourself, am I worth my time? And the only answer is Yes!

And what if those actions don't work out, or you fail? What then?

Then the cycle begins again. Start again, with baby steps. Look at what your expectations were that you were trying to fulfil, maybe simplify it. But don't give up, because that would mean you are giving up on yourself, and you don't want to give up on yourself, otherwise you wouldn't have picked up this book and read this far.

Keep trying, keep altering the goal until you do find something that works for you.

Persistence and consistency is the key. We only truly fail when we stop trying.

As long as you stay true to how you feel and take action that is committed and wholehearted and not doubting, you will at the very least learn something that will help you try again and be successful.

This is not a one time deal.

You choose to give yourself a second chance every time.

You choose to decide you are worth it.

Life is trial and error. We grow and learn through the errors.

But until you stop listening to the doubts and actually take action on what you believe you are capable of, you will never know.

Are you worth the risk? The longer you dawdle over the answer and don't take action, the more room you leave for self doubt.

Tuning into yourself and listening to what you feel about all sorts of things, including your fears and the things you want to change in your life, is how we undermine that negative chatter. Because once we know our truth and what we really feel about something, it can no longer be influenced by outside events or people. The goblins no longer have anything to feed off. We become secure in who we are and have that to build on.

Finding your balance

"Balance is the key to everything. What we do, think, say, eat, feel, they all require awareness, and through this aware-ness we can grow."
Koi Fresco

Some people believe that if they are not happy all the time there is something wrong with them – or in their relationship, friendships, job; that if things aren't working out the way they expected they are doing something wrong, or failing in some way. They don't believe it is okay to have an 'off' day and find life a struggle. They have to talk about being happy ALL the time and only say and do positive things – nothing negative will be tolerated (see the chapter on Toxic Positivity).

But this is not realistic. It's an 'all or nothing' mindset: 'I'm either bursting with joy or there's something wrong with me'.

But the trick to riding the pendulum of life is not to let it swing erratically. You have to find the balance.

A friend of mine asked me recently why it was that everyone around her seemed so happy all the time when she wasn't. She expressed how hard it was to keep up the pretence that she was happy too, just to fit in. But I reminded her that it was an illusion and that it was unlikely they were happy all the time. It was an assumption she was making that reflected her own feelings of anxiety about not feeling happy all the time. She believed she 'should' be happy all the time, yet inside her feelings didn't reflect that.

Many of us do this. I have often looked at others and their lives and felt envy, wondering how they were so content and happy. Asking myself, how have they achieved that? What am I doing wrong? But in reality I was projecting the thought that others were happier than me to sustain the cycle of misery and feelings of failure I was experiencing. When I spoke to those people I found their lives were not as perfect as I had thought – and some of those people felt the same way I did.

These feelings keep you disconnected, and can cause you to distance yourself, even withdraw from social interaction.

But separation causes pain; it is through connection that you feel love and a sense of belonging, both things vital to human well-being.

If you wake up one morning not feeling either happy or sad, don't push yourself to feel any particular way. You can let the day unfold, accept how you are feeling that day and in that moment, without any demands, and be gentle with yourself if things don't go the way you want them to by being compassionate to your feelings: listening to them, allow them to be felt, but don't expect anything from them.

If you are angry about something or at someone, allow yourself a moment to express it (alone by yourself preferably), let it out! Give yourself a chance to experience it, even laugh about it, and then return to yourself. If you feel upset or sad about something, again express it, say the comforting things you wish someone would say to you. Allow yourself to feel it and be there for yourself.

You have to accept that some days you might not wake up feeling full of energy, or looking forward to the day. And during those times it's okay to feel sad or overwhelmed and disappointed with life. The trick is to not hold onto it and think that it'll be like that forever. It is just a moment.

And that's all life is: a series of moments. And the more good moments you can create the better. But to expect them all to be great is where it falls down – or expect them all to be awful. Neither is true or real.

To find balance you need to connect to yourself and to those around you in that moment. If you speak your feelings out loud and be honest about them, and share them, you can stop seeking unattainable highs through self-imagined ideals of other people's lives.

By reducing expectations – both from yourself and from others – you can start living in the moment, whilst allowing yourself the 'bad days' and not push yourself to some unrealistic, insincere emotion.

Once you take the pressure off by not expecting something from yourself, you allow yourself to live a more balanced life.

I'm not saying it's easy; it takes consistent awareness of how you are feeling – I don't say constant because it's not possible to spend every waking moment aware of your feelings while getting on with your day-to-day life, but checking in with them regularly, or several times a day will aid this process. And at the same time giving those feelings room to be felt. They will pass, they just need to be acknowledged.

And note the word FEEL: it doesn't mean think through them, it means let them reside in your body. Acknowledge where they sit in your body (stomach, back, neck. chest, shoulders, jaw, etc.), what that feels like, then comfort and nurture them as you would a friend or a child, and eventually you will notice they reduce and pass.

Through this awareness you will find your own natural balance.

Recovering yourself

"I'm not telling you it's going to be easy – I'm telling you it's going to be worth it."
Art Williams

It's extremely difficult if you come from a broken or traumatic childhood to understand how to create inner happiness, or inner calm. It has taken me half a century to recover mine; to work out that I am a valuable person who does have something to contribute, and am worthy of honour and respect. And then to believe it. And from there grow a good feeling about myself inside. Because until we can create and hold a good feeling inside, it becomes infinitely more difficult to kill the goblins in the mind, which then taint everything externally.

As children we grow and learn from our parents and guardians. We model and reflect what they teach us. If they don't provide examples of positive things, like being content or satisfied, happy or safe, or even just calm, it can be difficult to manifest any of those things for ourselves. They are simply an unknown quantity which we have to teach ourselves later – once we become aware they are missing.

Before that point though, we imagine a good feeling being something that is generated externally by being successful in whatever we dream about doing or being in the world. We believe it will bring us the attention, respect or value we are missing inside. We attempt to do those things: be successful in business or a career, raise a family, but along the way we keep making compromises because we want to fit in and belong, and feel like there is a place for us in the world. And yet we still don't feel content or happy inside, we still feel churned up, or anxious, or whatever negative feeling dominated our formative years.

A certain level of disruption during childhood will create negative feelings that we get used to and then later maintain through creating or repeating similar drama in our own lives, because feeling any different is alien and feels wrong or uncomfortable.

If home life has been unsafe and full of fear it's hard to imagine it being anything else. You see others living a life where they appear happy and content, and you envy it because you don't know how to achieve that safe, settled feeling, because you've never experienced it.

We literally have to re-parent ourselves to recover our true selves, and we do that with nurturing and comfort and buckets of compassion and forgiveness – for ourselves, not anyone else.

The goblins are really all the voices of pain you suffered, all screaming at you to notice yourself. All the voices that are too scared to admit the truth about who you really are: a strong, vibrant light, someone of value and worth, who deserves and has a right to exist and be loved.

And until you start to believe that truth, feel that truth inside you, allow yourself to acknowledge and cherish that part of you, you will struggle to recover that true self inside.

And from that true self inside lies your happiness, your sense of belonging, your love – for yourself as well as those around you.

It starts with you.

And there are religions and belief systems which tell you that considering yourself is selfish, that seeking your own happiness is a bad thing. But those people or organisations are about getting you to succumb to their ideals and ways of thinking and believing. They will make you feel bad to entrap you and make you feel wretched unless you are thinking or believing what they tell you, you should be thinking and believing to serve their ways and systems.

But the truth is you were worthy the second you were born. You don't have to prove it to anyone, or be in service to anyone to make yourself worthy. Society might have tainted how you think about yourself, but you can recover it. And your happiness is important because not only does it feed you, it feeds those around you, those you love and take care of, creating a warm loving place.

If we all knew that we were innately valuable and worthy, how different would the world be? We could pursue the things we enjoy and matter to us, and come from a place of love all the time. We would be less consumed with having things to boost or pretend our value; we would be living from a heartfelt place.

And although that might sound like an unreachable utopia, it can happen in the world you create for yourself, within, and that in turn will project outwards and change your world.

What is therapy?

"The trouble with most therapy is that it helps you feel better, but you don't get better. You have to back it up with action, action, action."
Albert Ellis

A lot of people have said to me, therapy doesn't work for them. I always find that a curious statement.

The biggest misunderstanding about therapy is that going to see someone regularly will suddenly solve all your life problems; that it will magically change you and make you feel better. But that's not what happens.

Before I go into further detail, I want to go over exactly what I am referring to here. Therapy is 'talk therapy' where you go to someone on a regular basis and talk with them about what is going on with you.

There is a defined different between a psychologist and a psychiatrist, both of which can provide therapy. A psychologist will help you with changing how you think, your patterns and behaviours, whereas a psychiatrist will assess and diagnose your problems and provide medication to treat you.

And the country you are in will also dictate what is available to you and what you can afford. I've been extremely lucky in that I haven't paid much because the countries I have lived in while undertaking treatment (United Kingdom and The Netherlands) have had it covered in their medical care.

I have never been to a psychiatrist, I have only seen psychologists. I have had three different psychologists, each of them focused on helping me on specific issues.

My first therapy was for panic attacks, and I learnt about how my mind escalated my fears until they manifested into these attacks, which for me happened every night for over six months.

I didn't particularly like my first therapist. I found her very unsympathetic, and often I would come away feeling bad about myself, sometimes due to the things we talked about as it brought up a lot of emotions to do with past trauma; sometimes because I found her dismissive. But she provided me with the tools I needed to recover from the continuous panic attacks. And that meant that I had to do the work — me. Not her. Just me.

I would discuss it with her of course, but I had to understand the patterns in my mind and how to interrupt them and change them. It was hard, and took persistence, and even after the therapy sessions it took a couple of years, but it worked. Liking her and getting on with her had no part in my being able to implement the help she gave me.

I was surprised, however, when I returned to my doctor later, seeking further treatment, that the report she had sent to him expressed that she had only put a bandage on a much deeper problem. She had understood more than I thought.

My next therapist was much more approachable. He used a book called Staying Okay, by Thomas and Amy Harris, which follows a certain method called Transactional Analysis, to help me work through the abuse from my childhood. Again, I had to do the work: write out things, think about things, process things and become conscious of what I was thinking and doing. Eventually my therapist moved away to another country, so it stopped.

About fourteen years later I sought therapy again. This time for a breakdown, triggered by a succession of traumatic and physically painful events which resulted in me being in a very dark place in my head – 'black thinking' I call it, where I get stuck in suicidal ideation and struggle to get out of it. However, I was conscious of it and able to seek therapy.

This time I saw a psychologist that used a 'mindfulness' approach, and I saw him for six years, initially attending every week, and by the end just once a month.

What did he do? He would simply ask me how I was, and I would chatter away about how I was feeling, what was going on in my life, what things were coming up for me, and he would sort of guide some of my perspectives and pick things out for closer examination. He'd occasionally comment that I had already done a lot of work. And I had. I am an avid self-help book reader, and have always been open to trying out new ways of thinking about things.

And really that is what therapy is about: talking about your problems, finding a way to process them in your mind and view them from a different perspective.

At the end of the day the only person who got me to where I am is me. I did all the facing the issues, processing the issues and understanding the issues and how to change them in my mind.

So if therapy doesn't work for you, you can try another therapist, but ask yourself what are you expecting therapy to do for you?

It's extremely helpful to go in with an intention, even if it is, 'I want to stop feeling this way', or, 'I don't know how to deal with this.'

If you know what you need help with you have a starting point.

And the very fact you have turned up to therapy means that you are willing and open to find a new way to think and process things.

You can't change anything you don't acknowledge.

Because at the end of the day the quality of your internal life is down to you.

Only you can change your mind and feelings, no one else.

That is the one thing that is always within your power.

Recommended reading

I read a lot of self-help and personal development books. These are a few that really made a difference for me personally and which I recommend.

Erroneous Zone, by Dr Wayne Dyer

Wayne Dyer was a therapist and counsellor, who also became a bestselling author. This is my favourite of his books, and the one I most refer to, but Dr Wayne Dyer has a lot of books and guides. I also recommend **Pulling your Own Strings**.

Unlimited Power, by Tony Robbins

Tony Robbins is probably the most famous personal development and motivational speaker. He makes being able to change how you think and live your life accessible to everyone. This particular book helps you understand how to take control of your thinking and be successful in life. A real eye opener.

The Six Pillars of Self-Esteem, by Nathaniel Branden

This provides not only detailed information about how to raise your self-esteem, but also provides a simple daily course to help you in the back of the book. I found it revealing and helpful.

You are the One, by Kute Blackson

I have followed Kute for a few years now and love the subjects he talks on, which are very much based in self-love and how to find the real you. This book made me really understand how much we limit ourselves and our thinking, and showed me how to change that. It's a personal favourite, and might even be the only book I have read cover to cover multiple times.

Mirror Work, by Louise Hay

If you struggle with self-love and feeling valuable this book helps you work through the process of attaining those feelings within yourself first. Louise Hay is the founder of Hay House Publishing who publish the majority of everything in the self-help and personal development arena.

Braving the Wilderness, by Brene Brown

Brene Brown is a leader in talking on many subjects: vulnerability, courage, shame and empathy. But this book attracted me as it deals with how to feel true belonging. It is relevant to today's world and helped me understand many things about myself and society.

The Highly Sensitive Person, by Elaine N Aron

As I have a highly sensitive child, I was drawn to this book when I realised I was also a highly sensitive person. Not everyone is, but I found this really helpful when understanding my emotions. And the book **The Highly Sensitive Person in Love** helped me understand my relationships.

Staying OK by Amy & Thomas Harris

My therapist used this book for the basic structure and premise of his counselling. It helped me understand my feelings as well as how to backtrack triggered feelings and update core beliefs. Thomas Harris also wrote **I'm OK – You're OK**.

More book recommendations and reviews
can be found on my website:
www.mirandakrecoveringyourcalm.com

Author's Thanks

As this is my first foray into non-fiction, my usual writing support group was somewhat smaller for this topic, but there was one person who was always there for me, and even partner in helping me bring this together, Victoria Pearson. Without you there to help me brainstorm ideas and be a sounding board this book wouldn't have happened.

Also thanks to my betareaders, Lisa and Jemima. I was on tenterhooks but your responses made me realise it was worth my time.

My editor and proofreader, Michael. Where would I be without you?

Thanks in part also to the many therapists who have helped me recover a sense of myself, in particular Mr Roelofs who spent six years helping me work things out.

And, of course, thanks to my husband, Ron who allows me to sit at home and write these books, while taking care of our two children, as he goes out to work.

About the author

Miranda K is a British fiction and non-fiction author, who resides in the Netherlands. A veteran of childhood trauma, who, after years of inner emotional turmoil throughout her adult life, started a journey to recover herself, and her inner peace and security. Along the way she developed many tools, and discovered a lot about trauma, some of which she thought would be helpful to others.

You can find out more on her website, and even sign up to her newsletter.

www.mirandakrecoveringyourcalm.com

www.ingramcontent.com/pod-product-compliance
Lightning Source LLC
LaVergne TN
LVHW042157190726